AF225733

Accounting for
Intangible Assets

Steven M. Bragg

Table of Contents

About the Author

Steven Bragg, CPA, has been the chief financial officer or controller of four companies, as well as a consulting manager at Ernst & Young. He received a master's degree in finance from Bentley College, an MBA from Babson College, and a Bachelor's degree in Economics from the University of Maine. He has been a two-time president of the Colorado Mountain Club, and is an avid alpine skier, mountain biker, and certified master diver. Mr. Bragg resides in Centennial, Colorado. He has written more than 300 books and courses, including *New Controller Guidebook*, *GAAP Guidebook*, and *Payroll Management*.

Steven maintains the accountingtools.com web site, which contains continuing professional education courses, the Accounting Best Practices podcast, and thousands of articles on accounting subjects.

Buy Additional AccountingTools Courses

AccountingTools offers more than 1,500 hours of CPE courses, with concentrations in accounting, auditing, finance, taxation, and ethics. Related courses that you might like include:

- Business Valuation
- Fixed Asset Accounting
- GAAP Guidebook

Go to accountingtools.com/cpe to view these additional courses.

Accounting for Intangible Assets

Introduction

An intangible asset is a non-physical asset having a useful life that spans more than one accounting period. Examples of intangible assets are as follows:

<u>Marketing-related intangible assets</u>

- Trademarks
- Newspaper mastheads
- Internet domain names
- Noncompetition agreements

<u>Customer-related intangible assets</u>

- Customer lists
- Order backlog
- Customer relationships

<u>Artistic-related intangible assets</u>

- Performance events
- Literary works
- Musical works
- Pictures
- Motion pictures and television programs

<u>Contract-based intangible assets</u>

- Licensing agreements
- Service contracts
- Lease agreements
- Franchise agreements
- Broadcast rights
- Employment contracts
- Use rights (such as drilling rights or water rights)

<u>Technology-based intangible assets</u>

- Patented technology
- Computer software
- Trade secrets (such as secret formulas and recipes)

Another intangible asset is goodwill, which is recognized by an acquirer as part of an acquisition. Goodwill is the difference between the price paid for an acquiree and the fair value of all assets and liabilities of the acquiree that were purchased as part of the business combination. In essence, goodwill is the excess paid over the amount that should have been paid just for identifiable assets and liabilities.

In this manual, we deal with the accounting for goodwill after its initial recognition, and also address the accounting for and disclosure of the costs of several types of intangible assets, including other intangible assets, patents, internal-use software, and website development costs.

> **Related Podcast Episodes:** Episodes 136, 146, 175, and 189 of the Accounting Best Practices Podcast discuss goodwill impairment testing, intangible asset impairment testing, goodwill amortization, and accounting for acquired intangible assets, respectively. They are available at: **www.accountingtools.com/podcasts** or **iTunes**

Goodwill

Goodwill is a common byproduct of a business combination, where the purchase price paid for the acquiree is higher than the fair values of the identifiable assets acquired. See the author's *Business Combinations and Consolidations* book for more information about how goodwill is initially recognized.

After goodwill has initially been recorded as an asset, do not amortize it (with the exception noted in the Goodwill Amortization section). Instead, test it for impairment at the reporting unit level. Impairment exists when the carrying amount of the goodwill is greater than its implied fair value.

A reporting unit is defined as an operating segment or one level below an operating segment. At a more practical level, a reporting unit is a separate business for which the parent compiles financial information, and for which management reviews the results. If several components of an operating segment have similar economic characteristics, they can be combined into a reporting unit. In a smaller business, it is entirely possible that one reporting unit could be an entire operating segment, or even the entire entity.

The examination of goodwill for the possible existence of impairment involves a multi-step process, which is:

1. *Assess qualitative factors.* Review the situation to see if it is necessary to conduct further impairment testing, which is considered to be a likelihood of more than 50% that impairment has occurred, based on an assessment of relevant events and circumstances. Examples of relevant events and circumstances that make it more likely that impairment is present are:

    - *Macroeconomic conditions deteriorate.* For example, there can be a decline in general economic conditions, greater difficulty in accessing funding, or significant fluctuations in foreign exchange rates.

- *Industry deterioration.* For example, the level of competition increases, regulations become more stringent, or the market for the company's products declines.
- *Costs increase.* For example, increases in the costs of labor and/or materials are resulting in a profitability decline.
- *Financial performance declines.* For example, actual results decline below expectations, or decline in comparison to prior period results.
- *Negative impact on reporting unit.* An event has occurred that impacts a reporting unit, such as the recognition of a goodwill impairment loss by a subsidiary.
- *Share price decline.* There is a sustained drop in the price of the company's stock, either in relation to the share prices of peer entities or in absolute terms.
- *Other items.* There may be turnover in the management team, the loss of key personnel, or the arrival of a lawsuit against the organization.

If impairment appears to be likely, continue with the impairment testing process. The accountant can choose to bypass this step and proceed straight to the next step.

2. *Identify potential impairment.* Compare the fair value of the reporting unit to its carrying amount. If the fair value is greater than the carrying amount of the reporting unit, there is no goodwill impairment, and there is no need to proceed to the next step. If the carrying amount exceeds the fair value of the reporting unit, recognize an impairment loss in the amount of the difference, up to a maximum of the entire carrying amount (i.e., the carrying amount of goodwill can only be reduced to zero). One should consider the income tax effect from any tax deductible goodwill on the carrying amount of the entity (or the reporting unit), if applicable, when measuring the goodwill impairment loss.

These steps are illustrated in the following flowchart.

Goodwill Impairment Decision Steps

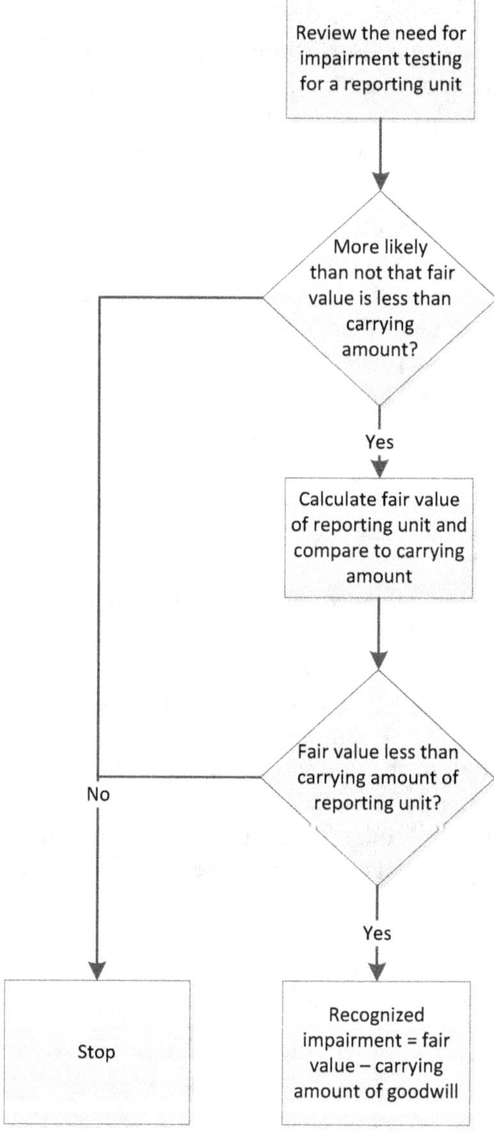

The fair value of the reporting unit is assumed to be the price that the company would receive if it were to sell the unit in an orderly transaction (i.e., not a rushed sale) between market participants. Other alternatives to the quoted market price for a reporting unit may be acceptable, such as a valuation based on multiples of earnings or revenue.

The following additional issues are associated with goodwill impairment testing:

- *Asset and liability assignment.* Assign acquired assets and liabilities to a reporting unit if they relate to the operations of the unit *and* they will be considered in the determination of reporting unit fair value. If these criteria can be met, even corporate-level assets and liabilities can be assigned to a reporting unit. If some assets and liabilities could be assigned to multiple reporting units, assign them in a reasonable manner (such as an allocation based on the relative fair values of the reporting units), consistently applied.
- *Asset recognition.* It is not allowable to recognize an additional intangible asset as part of the process of evaluating goodwill impairment.
- *Goodwill assignment.* All of the goodwill acquired in a business combination must be assigned to one or several reporting units as of the acquisition date, and not shifted among the reporting units thereafter. The assignment should be in a reasonable manner, consistently applied. If goodwill is to be assigned to a reporting unit that has not been assigned any acquired assets or liabilities, the assignment could be based on the difference between the fair value of the reporting unit before and after the acquisition, which represents the improvement in value caused by goodwill.
- *Impairment estimation.* If it is probable that there is goodwill impairment and the amount can be reasonably estimated, despite the testing process not being complete when financial statements are issued, recognize the estimated amount of the impairment. The estimate should be adjusted to the final impairment amount in the following reporting period.
- *No reversal.* Once impairment of goodwill has been recorded, it cannot be reversed, even if the condition originally causing the impairment is no longer present.
- *Reporting structure reorganization.* If a company reorganizes its reporting units, reassign assets and liabilities to the new reporting units based on a reasonable methodology, consistently applied. Goodwill should be reassigned based on the relative fair values of the portions of the old reporting unit to be integrated into the new reporting units.
- *Reporting unit disposal.* If a reporting unit is disposed of, include the goodwill associated with that unit in determining any gain or loss on the transaction. If only a portion of a reporting unit is disposed of, associate some of the goodwill linked to the reporting unit to the portion being disposed of, based on the relative fair values of the portions being disposed of and retained. Then test the remaining amount of goodwill assigned to the residual portion of the reporting unit for impairment.

EXAMPLE

Armadillo Industries is selling off a portion of a reporting unit for $500,000. The remaining portion of the unit, which Armadillo is retaining, has a fair value of $1,500,000. Based on these values, 25% of the goodwill associated with the reporting unit should be included in the carrying amount of the portion being sold.

- *Reporting unit disposal, minority owner.* If a company has less than complete ownership of a reporting unit, attribute any impairment losses to the parent entity and the noncontrolling interest in the reporting unit on a rational basis. However, if the reporting unit includes goodwill that is attributable to the parent entity, then attribute the loss entirely to the parent, not the noncontrolling interest.
- *Subsidiary goodwill impairment testing.* Any goodwill recognized by a corporate subsidiary should be dealt with in the same manner described elsewhere in this section for the impairment of goodwill. If there is a goodwill impairment loss at the subsidiary level, then also test the reporting unit of which that subsidiary is a part for goodwill impairment, if the triggering event is more likely than not to have also reduced the fair value of that reporting unit below its carrying amount.
- *Taxable transaction.* As part of the fair value estimation, determine whether the reporting unit could be bought or sold in a taxable or non-taxable transaction, since this affects its fair value.

Tip: From a practical perspective, it is almost always easier to estimate the fair value of the reporting unit based on a multiple of its earnings or revenues, though this should only be done when there are comparable operations whose fair values and related multiples are known, and which can therefore be used as the basis for a fair value estimate of the reporting unit.

Impairment testing is to be conducted at annual intervals. The impairment test may be conducted at any time of the year, provided that the test is conducted thereafter at the same time of the year. If the company is comprised of different reporting units, there is no need to test them all at the same time.

Tip: Each reporting unit is probably subject to a certain amount of seasonal activity. If so, select a period when activity levels are at their lowest to conduct impairment testing, so it does not conflict with other activities. Impairment testing should not coincide with the annual audit.

It may be necessary to conduct more frequent impairment testing if there is an event that makes it more likely than not that the fair value of a reporting unit has been reduced below its carrying amount. Examples of triggering events are a lawsuit, regulatory changes, the loss of key employees, and the expectation that a reporting unit will be sold.

> **Tip:** Private and non-profit entities only have to evaluate goodwill impairment triggering events as of the end of the reporting period. An entity that elects to take this approach does not have to monitor for goodwill impairment triggering events at other times.

The information used for an impairment test can be quite detailed. To improve the efficiency of the testing process, it is permissible to carry forward this information to the next year, as long as the following criteria have been met:

- There has been no significant change in the assets and liabilities comprising the reporting unit.
- There was a substantial excess of fair value over the carrying amount in the last impairment test.
- The likelihood of the fair value being less than the carrying amount is remote.

As an additional note for publicly-held companies that report segment information, the asset, liability, and goodwill allocations used for goodwill impairment testing do not have to be the same as the amounts stated in segment reports. However, aligning the two sets of information will make it easier to conduct both impairment testing and segment reporting.

Goodwill Amortization

The effort required to monitor the goodwill asset is considered to be excessive for private companies, while the usefulness of goodwill information is also considered to be limited. Consequently, a private company is allowed to amortize goodwill on a straight-line basis over a ten-year useful life. The entity may amortize goodwill over a shorter period if it can demonstrate that a shorter useful life is more appropriate. If an organization chooses to amortize goodwill, it must still test the goodwill asset for impairment at either the entity or reporting unit level. This test is triggered when there is an event that indicates a possible decline in the entity's or reporting unit's fair value to a point below its carrying amount. If an impairment loss is recognized, then any remaining carrying amount is to be amortized over its remaining useful life.

The amortization of goodwill will eventually reduce the carrying amount of an organization's goodwill asset so much that goodwill impairment will be quite unlikely, thereby reducing the need to spend time on such testing.

> **Note:** This goodwill amortization option is also available to not-for-profit entities.

Intangible Assets Other than Goodwill

In general, costs should be recognized as expenses when incurred when related to internally developing, maintaining, or restoring intangible assets that have any of the following characteristics:

- There is no specifically identifiable asset
- The useful life is indeterminate
- The cost is inherent in the continuing operation of the business

Conversely, it is possible to recognize an *acquired* intangible item as an asset. If a group of assets is acquired in a transaction that is not defined as a business combination, the acquisition cost should be entirely allocated to the individual acquired assets, based on their relative fair values. In such an arrangement, goodwill is not recognized.

In a business combination, it is entirely possible that an acquirer will recognize assets and liabilities that the acquiree had never recorded in its own accounting records. In particular, the acquirer will likely assign value to a variety of intangible assets that the acquiree may have developed internally, and so was constrained by generally accepted accounting principles from recognizing as assets. Examples of these intangible assets were noted in the introduction.

If a business acquires an intangible asset specifically to deny its use to others, this is called a defensive intangible asset. Treat this asset as a separate asset, rather than charging it to expense. Assign the asset a useful life that reflects the period over which the company will benefit from the denial of use of the asset to others; this period is essentially the period over which the fair value of the asset will decline.

The general accounting for an intangible asset is to record the asset as a long-term asset and amortize the asset over its useful life, along with regular impairment reviews. The accounting is essentially the same as for other types of fixed assets. The key differences between the accounting for tangible and intangible fixed assets are:

- *Amortization*. If an intangible asset has a useful life, amortize the cost of the asset over that useful life, less any residual value. Amortization is the same as depreciation, except that amortization is applied only to intangible assets. In this context, useful life refers to the time period over which an asset is expected to enhance future cash flows.
- *Residual value*. If any residual value is expected following the useful life of an intangible asset, subtract it from the carrying amount of the asset for the purposes of calculating amortization. One should assume that the residual value will always be zero for intangible assets, unless there is a commitment from another party to acquire the asset at the end of its useful life, *and* the residual value can be determined by reference to transactions in an existing market, *and* that market is expected to be in existence when the useful life of the asset ends.
- *Single unit of accounting*. If several intangible assets are operated as a single asset, combine them for the purposes of impairment testing. This treatment is

probably not suitable if they independently generate cash flows, would be sold separately, or are used by different asset groups.

EXAMPLE

Armadillo Industries purchases a patent from a third party. The remaining life of the patent's coverage of a key piece of production technology is eight years. Armadillo obtains a written commitment from a supplier to buy the patent in two years for 75% of the $100,000 price paid by Armadillo for the patent. Armadillo intends to sell the patent to the supplier in two years.

Based on this information, Armadillo should amortize $25,000 of the purchase price over the two years that the company expects to retain ownership of the patent.

[see the Patents section for more information about the accounting for patents]

- *Useful life*. An intangible asset may have an indefinite useful life. If so, do not initially amortize it, but review the asset at regular intervals to see if a useful life can then be determined. If so, test the asset for impairment and begin amortizing it. The reverse can also occur, where an asset with a useful life is judged to now have an indefinite useful life; if so, stop amortizing the asset and test it for impairment. Examples of intangible assets that have indefinite useful lives are taxicab licenses, broadcasting rights, and trademarks.

EXAMPLE

Milford Sound acquires a license to broadcast in the Milwaukee area for five years. The license is automatically renewable every five years, unless Milford violates a number of Federal Communications Commission rules. There is no limit to the number of renewals that Milford can obtain to the license period, and Milford intends to renew the license in perpetuity. Despite the impact of music streaming over the Internet, the cash flows associated with the license are not expected to decline appreciably in the foreseeable future. Thus, the cash flows that Milford expects to realize from the license should continue indefinitely. The license can be treated as an intangible asset having an indefinite useful life.

- *Useful life revisions*. The duration of the remaining useful lives of all intangible assets should be regularly reviewed, and adjusted if circumstances warrant the change. This will require a change in the remaining amount of amortization recognized per period. The determination of the correct useful life is based on a number of factors, including the following:
  - o The expected use of the asset
  - o The expected useful life of another asset to which the intangible asset is related
  - o Any legal provisions that limit the useful life
  - o The entity's history of being able to extend the life of similar assets

- o The effects of economic factors, such as competition and demand
- o The amount of maintenance costs needed to obtain future cash flows, where high costs indicate a limited useful life

- *Life extensions.* It is possible that the life of some intangible assets may be extended a considerable amount, usually based on contract extensions. If so, estimate the useful life of an asset based on the full duration of expected useful life extensions. These presumed extensions may result in an asset having an indefinite useful life, which avoids amortization.

EXAMPLE

Milford Sound entered into a license for noise cancelling technology three years ago, and plans to renew the license for an additional three-year period. However, management is aware of the development of a new technology that will probably render the current noise cancelling technology obsolete in two years. Milford had previously been amortizing the cost of the license over each three-year licensing period. Given the expected change in technology, management elects to amortize the cost of the license extension over just two years.

- *Straight-line amortization.* Use the straight-line basis of amortization to reduce the carrying amount of an intangible asset, unless the pattern of benefit usage associated with the asset suggests a different form of amortization.

Tip: The usage pattern of nearly all intangible assets will suggest the use of straight-line amortization. Since this is also the simplest amortization method, use it unless the underlying usage pattern of an asset is substantially different.

- *Impairment testing.* An intangible asset is subject to impairment testing in the same manner as tangible assets. In short, recognize impairment if the carrying amount of the asset is greater than its fair value, and the amount is not recoverable. Once recognized, the impairment cannot be reversed. In the assessment of impairment, review all events and circumstances that could affect the determination of fair value, such as:
  - o Increases in costs that could negatively impact earnings and cash flows
  - o Declines in actual or planned revenue
  - o Regulatory, legal, contractual and other factors that limit fair value
  - o Litigation
  - o Management changes or the loss of key personnel
  - o Decline in the business environment or general economic conditions

- *Research and development assets.* If intangible assets are acquired by a not-for-profit entity through a business combination for use in research and development activities, initially treat them as having indefinite useful lives, and regularly test them for impairment. Once the related research and development activities have been completed or abandoned, charge them to expense.

Internal-Use Software

Companies routinely develop software for internal use, and want to understand how these development costs are to be accounted for. Software is considered to be for internal use when it has been acquired or developed *only* for the internal needs of a business. Examples of situations where software is considered to be developed for internal use are:

- Accounting systems, such as for billings, payables, and payroll
- Cash management tracking systems
- Database and case management systems
- Membership tracking systems
- Product design systems
- Production automation systems

Conversely, examples of situations in which software is *not* developed for internal use are:

- Software used by consumers to run a company's products
- Software embedded in computer chips that are included in products
- Software that is sold as a standalone product

Further, there can be no reasonably possible plan to market the software outside of the company. A market feasibility study is not considered a reasonably possible marketing plan. However, a history of selling software that had initially been developed for internal use creates a reasonable assumption that the latest internal-use product will also be marketed for sale outside of the company.

The accounting for internal-use software varies, depending upon the stage of completion of the project. The relevant accounting is:

- *Stage 1: Preliminary.* All costs incurred during the preliminary stage of a development project should be charged to expense as incurred. This stage is considered to include making decisions about the allocation of resources, determining performance requirements, conducting supplier demonstrations, evaluating technology, and supplier selection.
- *Stage 2: Application development.* Capitalize the costs incurred to develop internal-use software, which may include coding, hardware installation, and testing. Any costs related to data conversion, user training, administration, and overhead should be charged to expense as incurred. Only the following costs can be capitalized:
    - o Materials and services consumed in the development effort, such as third party development fees, software purchase costs, and travel costs related to development work.

       o   The payroll costs of those employees directly associated with software development.

       o   The capitalization of interest costs incurred to fund the project.

- *Stage 3. Post-implementation.* Charge all post-implementation costs to expense as incurred. Samples of these costs are training and maintenance costs.

Any allowable capitalization of costs should begin *after* the preliminary stage has been completed, management commits to funding the project, it is probable that the project will be completed, and the software will be used for its intended function.

The capitalization of costs should end when all substantial testing has been completed. If it is no longer probable that a project will be completed, stop capitalizing the costs associated with it, and conduct impairment testing on the costs already capitalized. The cost at which the asset should then be carried is the lower of its carrying amount or fair value (less costs to sell). Unless there is evidence to the contrary, the usual assumption is that uncompleted software has no fair value.

A business may purchase software for internal use. If the purchase price of this software includes other elements, such as training and maintenance fees, only capitalize that portion of the purchase price that relates to the software itself.

In addition, any later upgrades of the software can be capitalized, but only if it is probable that extra system functionality will result from the upgrade. The costs of maintaining the system should be charged to expense as incurred. If the maintenance is provided by a third party and payment is made in advance for the services of that party, amortize the cost of the maintenance over the service period.

Once costs have been capitalized, amortize them over the expected useful life of the software. This is typically done on a straight-line basis, unless another method more clearly reflects the expected usage pattern of the software. Amortization should begin when a software module is ready for its intended use, which is considered to be when all substantial system testing has been completed. If a software module cannot function unless other modules are also completed, do not begin amortization until the related modules are complete.

It may be necessary to regularly reassess the useful life of the software for amortization purposes, since technological obsolescence tends to shorten it.

The capitalized cost of internal-use software should be routinely reviewed for impairment, as described earlier. The following are all indicators of the possible presence of asset impairment:

- The software is not expected to be of substantive use
- The manner in which the software was originally intended to be used has now changed
- The software is to be significantly altered
- The development cost of the software significantly exceeded original expectations

Once a business has developed software for internal use, management may decide to market it for external use by third parties. If so, the proceeds from software licensing, net of selling costs, should be applied against the carrying amount of the software asset. For the purposes of this topic, selling costs are considered to include commissions, software reproduction costs, servicing obligations, warranty costs, and installation costs. The business should not recognize a profit on sales of the software until the application of net sales to the carrying amount of the software asset has reduced the carrying amount to zero. The business can recognize all further proceeds as revenue.

The guidance noted in this section is identical for the fees paid by a customer in a cloud computing arrangement (where software and/or data are being hosted on the systems of a third party). In this situation, capitalized implementation costs are ratably charged to expense over the term of the hosting arrangement.

> **Related Podcast Episode:** Episode 270 of the Accounting Best Practices Podcast discusses the accounting for software as a service (SaaS) from the perspectives of both the customer and the service provider. The episode is available at: **www.accountingtools.com/podcasts** or **iTunes**

Website Development Costs

A company may allocate funds to the development of a company website, in such areas as coding, graphics design, the addition of content, and site operation. The accounting for website development varies, depending upon the stage of completion of the project. The relevant accounting is:

- *Stage 1: Preliminary.* Charge all site planning costs to expense as incurred. This stage is considered to include project planning, the determination of site functionality, hardware identification, technology usability, alternatives analysis, supplier demonstrations, and legal considerations.
- *Stage 2: Application development and infrastructure.* The accounting matches what was just described in the last section for internal-use software. In essence, capitalize these costs. More specifically, capitalize the cost of obtaining and registering an Internet domain, as well as the procurement of software tools, code customization, web page development, related hardware, hypertext link creation, and site testing. Also, if a site upgrade provides new functions or features to the website, capitalize these costs.
- *Stage 3: Graphics development.* For the purposes of this topic, graphics are considered to be software, and so are capitalized, unless they are to be marketed externally. Graphics development includes site page design and layout.
- *Stage 4: Content development.* Charge data conversion costs to expense as incurred, as well as the costs to input content into a website.
- *Stage 5: Site operation.* The costs to operate a website are the same as any other operating costs, and so should be charged to expense as incurred. The treatment of selected operating costs associated with a website are:
  - Charge website hosting fees to expense over the period benefited by the hosting

> o Charge search engine registration fees to expense as incurred, since they are advertising costs

Non-Fungible Tokens

A non-fungible token (NFT) is a cryptographic asset with a unique identification code. The concept is mostly applied to collectibles. There are no accounting standards yet that are specifically targeted at NFTs, but they would be classified as intangible assets. So, when you buy an NFT, just record it at its purchase price. According to GAAP, the recorded value of an intangible asset can't be increased, so the purchase price is the hard cap on the recorded value of the asset.

If the market value of an NFT declines, then you may have to record an impairment charge to reduce the initial purchase cost down to the current market value of similar assets. Valuing an NFT can be difficult. You could use a comparison based on the prices at which similar assets are currently trading. Another possibility is deriving a present value for the expected future stream of earnings associated with an NFT – if there are any earnings at all. Given the volatility of NFT prices, an impairment calculation would be based on the average trading price of a set of similar assets over perhaps the last couple of months – just to come up with some sort of reasonably stable market value.

Another issue is whether you should amortize an NFT. Probably not, since an NFT is assumed to have an indefinite lifespan, like a trademark. In this case, there is no point in recording a monthly amortization charge, since the NFT is expected to retain its value for an extremely long period of time.

The accounting is a bit different if you are the creator of an NFT. In this case, the amount for which it sells is immediately recorded as revenue, since there aren't any delayed obligations associated with the sale. And the sale price is probably going to be about the same as the related profit, since there won't be much in the way of expenses associated with the sale.

Patents

A patent is considered an intangible asset; this is because a patent does not have physical substance, and provides long-term value to the owning entity. As such, the accounting for a patent is the same as for any other intangible fixed asset, which is:

- *Initial recordation.* Record the cost to acquire the patent as the initial asset cost. If a company files for a patent application, this cost will include the registration, documentation, and other legal fees associated with the application. If the company instead bought a patent from another party, the purchase price is the initial asset cost.
- *Amortization.* The owner of the patent gradually charges the cost of the patent to expense over the useful life of the patent, usually using the straight-line amortization method.

- *Impairment*. If a patent no longer provides value, or a reduced level of value, recognize an impairment to reduce or eliminate the carrying amount of the asset.
- *Derecognition*. Once the company is no longer making use of the patented idea, the asset can be derecognized by crediting the balance in the patent asset account and debiting the balance in the accumulated amortization account. If the asset has not been fully amortized at the time of derecognition, then any remaining unamortized balance must be recorded as a loss.

Consider the following additional points when considered the accounting for patents:

- *R&D expenditures*. Note that the research and development (R&D) costs required to develop the idea being patented cannot be included in the capitalized cost of a patent. These R&D costs are instead charged to expense as incurred; the basis for this treatment is that R&D is inherently risky, without assurance of future benefits, so it should not be considered an asset.
- *Useful life*. A patent asset should not be amortized for longer than the life span of the protection afforded by the patent. If the expected useful life of the patent is even shorter, use the useful life for amortization purposes. Thus, the shorter of a patent's useful life and its legal life should be used for the amortization period.
- *Capitalization limit*. In practice, the costs of obtaining a patent may be so small that they do not meet or exceed a company's capitalization limit. If so, charge these costs to expense as incurred. In many larger companies with higher capitalization limits, this means that patents are rarely recorded as assets unless they have been purchased from other entities.

EXAMPLE

Pensive Corporate buys a patent from a competitor for $500,000. Pensive plans to use the patent for the next five years. The patent expires in 10 years. Since the five-year usage period is shorter than the legal life, Pensive should set the useful life of the patent at five years. This means the company will charge $100,000 to amortization expense in each of the next five years.

Intangibles Disclosures

A company that has recognized goodwill as an asset should disclose the following information in its financial statements:

- *Estimated impairment*. If a company recognizes an estimated amount of impairment in its financial statements, disclose the fact that the amount recognized is an estimate. In later periods, disclose the nature and amount of any significant adjustments made to the initial estimate.

- *Goodwill carrying amount.* Disclose a reconciliation of changes in the carrying amount of goodwill during the period, showing the beginning gross amount and accumulated impairment losses, additional goodwill recognition, adjustments for deferred tax assets, goodwill related to assets held for sale, impairment losses, other changes, and the ending gross amount and accumulated impairment losses.
- *Goodwill by segment.* If a company is reporting segment information (which is required for publicly-held companies), disclose the amount of goodwill in total, and for each reportable segment, as well as significant changes in the allocation of goodwill by segment.
- *Goodwill impairment activity.* If there has been goodwill impairment, present the related losses in a separate line item in the income statement, positioned before the subtotal of income from continuing operations. If the goodwill is associated with a discontinued operation, then present the loss, net of taxes, in a line item in the discontinued operations section of the income statement.
- *Goodwill impairment loss.* If there is a goodwill impairment loss, disclose the facts and circumstances associated with the loss, the amount of the loss, and how the fair value of the related reporting unit was determined.
- *Goodwill presentation.* State the aggregate amount of goodwill in a separate line item in the balance sheet. If goodwill is being amortized, then this amount should be presented net of the amortization.
- *Unallocated goodwill.* If any goodwill has not been allocated to a reporting unit, disclose the unallocated amount and the reasons why no allocation has been made.

EXAMPLE

Armadillo Industries discloses the following information about changes in the carrying amount of its goodwill for the year ended December 31, 20X4:

(000s)	Body Armor Segment	High Pressure Container Segment	Total
Balance as of January 1, 20X4			
Goodwill	$5,700	$4,200	$9,900
Accumulated impairment losses	-400	-170	-570
	5,300	4,030	9,330
Goodwill acquired during year	360	1,080	1,440
Impairment losses	-250	--	-250
Goodwill written off related to disposal of business unit	--	-200	-200
Balance as of December 31, 20X4			
Goodwill	6,060	5,080	11,140
Accumulated impairment losses	-650	-170	-820
	$5,410	$4,910	$10,320

The company tests the body armor segment in the second quarter of each year, which is the low point in the company's sales cycle. Due to an increase in lower-priced competition from Asian manufacturers, management revised its estimate of future cash flows likely to be generated by the body armor segment, and concluded that a goodwill impairment of $250,000 should be recognized. The fair value of the body armor reporting unit was derived using the expected present value of future cash flows.

A company that has recognized other intangible assets should disclose the following information in its financial statements:

- *Intangible presentation.* Aggregate all recognized intangible assets into one line in the balance sheet (though the breakdown of this information into additional lines is allowed).
- *Amortization expense.* Report amortization expense within the continuing operations section of the income statement.
- *Impairment losses.* Report intangible asset impairment losses within the continuing operations section of the income statement.
- *Acquired intangibles.* If intangible assets are acquired, disclose the following:
    - The amount assigned to the major intangible asset classes
    - The amount of any residual value (if significant) by asset class and in total
    - The weighted average amortization period by asset class
    - The total amount of intangible assets with indefinite lives, by asset class
    - The research and development asset cost acquired and written off (other than through a business combination), and the income statement line item where this information is located
    - The weighted-average period before the next terms extension, by asset class, for those assets having renewal terms

When a company presents a balance sheet as part of its financial statements, it should also disclose the following information:

- *Amortization expense.* Note the total amortization expense for the period.
- *Assets with indefinite lives.* List the total carrying amount of all intangible assets that are not subject to amortization, as well as the same information by asset class.
- *Extended assets.* For those assets whose lives have been renewed or extended in the period, state the amount of renewal costs capitalized by asset class, as well as the weighted-average period before the next renewal, by asset class.
- *Future amortization.* State the estimated amount of amortization expense in each of the next five fiscal years.
- *Goodwill amortization.* If the organization engages in goodwill amortization, disclose the gross carrying amounts of goodwill, accumulated amortization,

and accumulated impairment losses, as well as the aggregate amortization expense for the period. Additional disclosure is required for held-for-sale assets.

- *Impairment losses.* For each impairment loss recognized, disclose the period of recognition, the nature of the asset, the reasons for impairment, the amount of the loss, the method used to determine fair value, the income statement line item into which the loss is aggregated, and the segment in which the impaired asset is reported (only applicable to publicly-held companies).
- *Intangible asset totals.* State the gross carrying amount and related accumulated amortization for all intangible assets, and for each major asset class.
- *Life extension policy.* Describe the company policy for how it treats any costs incurred to renew the life of an intangible asset.
- *Renewal impact on cash flows.* Provide sufficient information for users to judge how cash flows will be affected by the ability of the business to renew the contractual life of an asset.

EXAMPLE

Armadillo Industries discloses the following information related to its acquisition of intangible assets:

Note X: Acquired Intangible Assets

(000s)	As of December 31, 20X1 Gross Carrying Amount	As of December 31, 20X1 Accumulated Amortization
Amortized intangible assets		
Customer list	$2,130	-$720
Internet domain names	1,600	-870
Trademarks	420	-380
Total	$4,150	-$1,970
Unamortized intangible assets		
Trade secrets	$4,350	
Trademarks	1,880	
Total	$6,230	

Aggregate amortization expense:	
For the year ended 12/31/20X1	$395
Estimated amortization expense:	
For the year ended 12/31/20X2	580
For the year ended 12/31/20X3	520
For the year ended 12/31/20X4	490
For the year ended 12/31/20X5	370

Summary

The testing for goodwill impairment can be both time-consuming and expensive, so take full advantage of the option to avoid testing by reviewing qualitative factors to see if there is a low likelihood of impairment.

Be aware of how the capitalization of software for internal use or for the development of a website can skew the results reported by a business. If a company is developing a massive in-house system, the amount of costs capitalized may represent a significant proportion of all expenditures, resulting in financial statements that may reveal a profit, even while the business is hemorrhaging cash to pay for the development effort. If this is the case, consider full disclosure of the situation in the company's financial statements, as well as a narrow interpretation of the accounting standards to charge as much of these expenditures as possible to expense as incurred.

Glossary

B

Business combination. A transaction in which the acquirer obtains control of another business (the acquiree).

D

Defensive intangible asset. An intangible asset that has been acquired specifically to deny its use to others.

G

Goodwill. The excess paid by an acquirer over the fair value of the acquired assets and liabilities.

I

Intangible asset. An asset that lacks physical substance.

N

Non-fungible token. A cryptographic asset with a unique identification code.

O

Operating segment. A component of an entity that is a profit center, has discrete financial information available, and whose results are reviewed regularly by the entity's chief operating decision maker.

R

Reporting unit. A separate business for which the parent compiles financial information, and for which management reviews the results.

Residual value. The estimated amount that an asset will be worth at the end of its useful life.

U

Useful life. The estimated lifespan of a depreciable fixed asset, during which it can be expected to contribute to company operations.

Index